A RADLAUER Model BOOK

WARSHIPS

by Ed Radlauer
Photographs by Ed and Ruth Radlauer

AN ELK GROVE BOOK
CHILDRENS PRESS, CHICAGO

**Created for Childrens Press
by Radlauer Productions, Incorporated**

Battleship *Bismarck*, pages 38 and 40, built by John Schertle of La Habra Heights, California.

All other models built by Sergeant Michael Castro, California Air National Guard.

Photo credits: Naval Photographic Center, pages 4 and 42

Library of Congress Cataloging in Publication Data

Radlauer, Ed.
    Warships.

    (A Radlauer model book)
    Includes index.
    Summary: An introduction to warships over the centuries to be used as a guide to building models. A glossary/index of related terms is included.
    1.   Ship models—Juvenile literature.   2.   Warships—Juvenile literature.   [1.   Warships—History.   2.   War-ships—Models.   3.   Ship models.   4.   Models and model-making]   I.   Radlauer, Ruth; 1926-   ill.   II.   Title.
VM298.R24   1984   623.8′2015   83-21035
ISBN 0-516-08013-X   ships - models
                              c

Contents

Warships

Galleys*
Galleons
Battleships
Nuclear power
Raiders
Cruisers

When did all this start?

*Words printed **like this (bold face)** are found in the Glossary/Index on pages 44-48.

No one really knows when people started using warships. We do know the warship story is long, interesting, and important. At first people probably used plain ships and boats for trade. After losing some of their traders to enemies, leaders decided they needed warships to protect their trade routes. Later people may have needed warships to protect themselves from enemies. Or they may have needed warships because leaders thought it was time for war.

No one really knows how **naval warfare*** started. Maybe it started when someone out on a fishing boat thought another person on a fishing boat was taking too many fish.

Yes, the story of warships is long and important. Let's look at some of the important models in this long story. Then you can build some models of your own. Our story starts with the model of a ship that sailed the seas many hundreds of years ago. The country was Rome, the time more than 3000 years ago.

*Words printed **like this (bold face)** are found in the Glossary/Index on pages 44-48.

Biremes

Country: *Rome*
Class: *Galley*
Time: *1100–1500* **B.C.**
Length: *50 feet*
Breadth: *25 feet*
Propulsion: *Wind, sail, slaves, oars*

Biremes, triremes, *quadriremes, and quinqueremes?*

Some Roman galley ships were named by how many slaves worked each oar. Two slaves per oar was a *bireme.* Three slaves, trireme. If there were four slaves at each oar, it was a *quadrireme.* And some ships had five slaves at each oar. That was a *quinquereme.* Of course, wind and sail could move Roman **merchant** ships very nicely. It seems the Romans were in a big hurry, so they added **galley slaves** to their warship propulsion systems.

The real reason the Romans used slaves at the oars is that during battle, the Romans took down the sails. With sails down and slaves rowing, a ship's captain could move into battle without worrying about which way the wind was blowing.

Now about the slaves. They weren't at all friendly with their masters. So the masters kept the slaves chained to the oars. And if the boat sank? Yes, that was bad news because the slaves went down with the boat.

Galleys also had a long pointed front called a **ram bow.** When the slaves got the galley going full speed, the Romans crashed their boat into an enemy ship and crunched a big hole in it. Then it was bad news for the enemy. They went down with their ship. The Romans don't sound very friendly, do they? But then, no country at war can be very friendly.

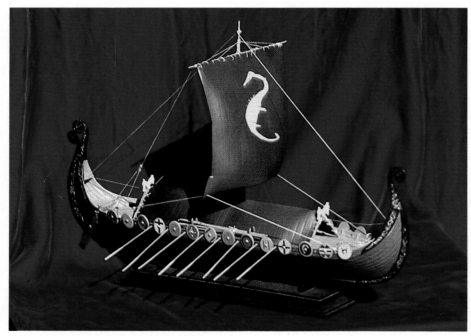

Viking Ships

Country: **Scandinavia**
Dates: *Possibly from 2000 B.C. to **A.D.** 650*
Length: *60–90 feet*
Breadth: *12–17 feet*
Propulsion: *Wind, sail, oars*
Armament: *Stones, bow and arrow, spears, swords, giant axes*

*Where did the **Viking ships** sail?*

The Scandinavians sailed their wooden ships great distances. Much sailing was coastwise. Some records show that the Vikings sailed their sturdy craft to places such as Iceland, Greenland, and even to America long before the time of Columbus. To sail these great distances, the Vikings needed **seaworthy** ships. They also needed to know a great deal about **navigation.**

For some reason, the Vikings built the ships to be the same at both ends. Maybe that was to keep the enemy from telling if a ship was coming or going.

One of their models was called a **longboat.** It could move through the water quietly. By moving quietly the crew on the long boat could surprise the enemy with stones, bows and arrows, spears, swords, and giant axes. When the enemy surrendered, the Vikings grabbed everything in sight to take home as **plunder.** Vikings don't sound like very friendly people. But then, during war, people just don't act friendly.

Galleons

Countries: *Portugal, England, Spain*
Dates: *Around A.D. 1300 to 1500*
Propulsion: *Wind, sail, and oars*
Armament: *Monster cannons*

Why were Spanish galleons so good at wrecking enemy ships but not at winning the battles?

Spanish galleons were taller than other ships of the time. That meant the galleon gunners could pour cannon fire down on an enemy **merchantman.** You see, the Spanish didn't want to sink the enemy ship. They just wanted to grab the ship and its cargo. Then they tossed the crew into the sea.

It worked like this. The Spanish galleon bombarded the merchantman into giving up. Then the Spanish sailors boarded the merchantman which had an unarmed crew. But sometimes the Spanish got a surprise. The merchantman had heavily armed sailors on board, and it was the Spanish sailors who got tossed into the sea instead.

Galleons had other problems. Their huge cannons had huge **recoils.** Sometimes the cannons exploded on board the ship. And more Spanish sailors fell into the sea.

No, the Spanish galleon was not the perfect weapon. Maybe there will never be one. But the galleons did set the style used in naval warfare for 350 years. This style of naval warfare didn't change a great deal until 400 years later when the aircraft carrier was invented.

U.S.S. Constitution (Old Ironsides)

Country: *United States of America*
Class: **Frigate**
Launched: *1797*
Length: *204 feet*
Breadth: *43.6 feet*
Propulsion: *Wind and sail*
Armament: *30–36 cannons*

Was there much iron in Old Ironsides?

Probably not. While your model of *Old Ironsides* is made of plastic, the real frigate, U.S.S. *Constitution,* was made of woods such as red cedar, live oak, and straight pine. The only iron in *Old Ironsides* was in the guns and heavy **anchor.** But the ship got the name *Old Ironsides* after winning battles against French and Barbary pirates and the British navy.

Life for sailors on board the *Constitution* was not easy. There was no good way to keep warm *or* cool. Food was either dried or salted. How do you like this menu? Salt beef, bread; salt pork, dried peas, bread; rice, cheese, molasses, vinegar, **suet,** and bread.

As a sailor on the *Constitution,* you had a space 22 inches wide and eight feet long to set up your **hammock** and sleep.

But **hardships** on this ship or not, the U.S.S. *Constitution was* the beginning of the gallant United States Navy.

U.S.S. Olympia

Country: *United States of America*
Class: ***Raiding cruiser***
Service: *Early 1900s*
Propulsion: *Steam*

Let's raid enemy **commerce.**

Why raid enemy commerce? Because without commerce the enemy could starve, run out of **war materiel,** or just plain run out of money to keep a war going.

So the early raiding cruisers such as the U.S.S. *Olympia* were fast and lightweight. They could strike at the enemy and then use their high speed to get away before the enemy could strike back.

In time of war, raiding cruisers could be used as light battleships. They could also act as **scouts** for battleships and other **vessels** in the **fleet.** The *Olympia* had a good speed of between 24 to 26 **knots.** Later, when speed wasn't enough for protection against equally fast enemy ships, the raiding cruiser got some protection in the form of six-inch **armor plate.** In 1898, the U.S.S. *Olympia* was used against the Spanish in a place called Manila Bay in the Phillipine Islands. On May 1, 1898, the *Olympia* single-handedly destroyed 12 Spanish small cruisers and **gunboats.**

The perfect weapon? Some thought so. But in just a few years, the *Olympia* class was already **obsolete.** Well, in warfare we never know what's coming next, do we?

U.S.S. Arizona

Country: *United States of America*
Class: *Battleship,* Pennsylvania *class*
Launched: *June 19, 1915*
Top Speed: *21 knots*
Sunk: *December 7, 1941*

Will we ever forget the battleship U.S.S. Arizona?

No, we'll probably never forget the U.S.S. *Arizona*. Why? Because on December 7, 1941, the Japanese sank the U.S.S. *Arizona* while it was **moored** in Pearl Harbor, Hawaii. During this attack many other ships were sunk. But the *Arizona* sinking set a record. The record was to have 1177 people lost in the sinking of a single ship.

Before the attack on Pearl Harbor, the *Arizona* had a long and great history. In a way, she was really two ships. From 1915 to 1929 she was the Old *Arizona,* a good ship during the 1920s after World War I. Then, around 1930, the *Arizona* was **refitted.** The work took two years. During this time the *Arizona* got new gun **turrets,** new **boilers,** and aircraft **catapults.** For many years following the refitting, the *Arizona* sailed the seas doing the work of the proud United States Navy.

The end came when a Japanese **torpedo** hit the *Arizona* in the area of the **forward magazine** at 8:20 A.M. on December 7, 1941. The *Arizona* suffered a huge explosion and burned. By evening the *Arizona* was at the bottom of Pearl Harbor, and the United States was about to enter World War II. Many more ships from many nations would go to the bottom before the war ended in 1945.

PT Boat 109

Country: *United States of America*
Class: *Patrol torpedo boat (PT Boat)*
Launched: *July, 1942*
Propulsion: *Three twelve-cylinder engines*
Armament: *Four torpedo tubes, two twin .50 caliber machine guns, 20mm cannons*

Why is PT boat 109 more famous than other PT boats?

During World War II in the Pacific, all the fast PT boats were a little bit famous. With their three twelve-cylinder engines they could go zipping around, attacking enemy ships with their torpedoes. This kind of fight was called hit-and-run.

Since all the PT boats were good at hit-and-run attacks, why is PT boat 109 more famous than the others? Because one night while PT boats 109, 162, and 169 were sitting quietly in the water, waiting to attack, a Japanese ship rushed at PT 109, sliced it in half, and set it on fire. Some of the crew were killed. Other sailors were able to swim three and a half miles to an island. One of the men who made that four-hour swim was John F. Kennedy, who later became President of the United States. No wonder you're famous, PT Boat 109.

U.S.S. *Growler*

Country:	*United States of America*
Class:	***Conventionally-powered submarine***
Time:	*World War II*
Ships sunk:	*Ten*
Growler sunk:	*November 8, 1944*

Did the Growler have something to growl about and was it the number three?

Yes, the *Growler* was famous for the number three. In June of 1942 in the waters around Alaska, the *Growler* came upon three Japanese warships. What to do? The *Growler* fired at all three. One sank, the others were put out of service. People called that something to growl about.

But good luck ran out for the *Growler* on February 7, 1943. The captain and some of the crew were on the submarine's deck. All of a sudden, a Japanese boat showed up and crashed into the *Growler*. At the same time the Japanese started shooting at the submarine sailors on the deck. There were seven men on the deck, the captain and six crewmen. The captain ordered the sub to dive. Six of the men got into the submarine before it **submerged.** The captain was too late. He had saved the submarine by ordering it to dive. But in so doing he had given his own life.

Submarine people never forget the last words of the *Growler's* captain. Even though he knew it meant his death, he ordered, "Take her down!"

I-class Submarine

Country: *Japan*
Time: *World War II*
Range: *30,000 miles*
Length: *394 feet*

Did the huge I-class submarine carry a flying fish?

Yes, during World War II, you might say 40 of the Japanese I-class submarines did carry a kind of flying fish. The fish was an **amphibious reconnaissance** airplane that could also carry two small bombs. But what happened to the flying fish airplane while the **sub** traveled underwater? The sailors took the airplane apart and stored it in a **hangar** on the submarine deck.

When it was time to send the airplane out, usually in the early morning, sailors took the plane out, put it together, set it on a catapult, and sent it on its way. The plane could fly about three hours looking for targets the sub could attack. It could also drop a bomb or two if the pilot found a target.

When the plane got back to the sub, the pilot landed on the water and the Japanese sailors hauled the aircraft onto the submarine. Then they took it apart and put it back in its hangar for the night.

Sometimes the sub came under attack while the plane was being launched or recovered. Then what happened? Bye, bye, flying fish.

Yes many strange ideas have been tried during war times. Many more will be tried, we can be sure.

U.S.S. Missouri

Country: *United States of America*
Class: **Dreadnought**
Date: *World War II*
Displacement: *Around 70,000 tons*
Armament: *The biggest guns the ship can carry without sinking*

The idea of building a dreadnought class ship started in the year 1906. What was the idea?

Naval planners figured that in any battle between warships, the vessel with the biggest guns would be the winner. The dreadnought idea lasted through World War II when the *Missouri* was at sea doing **escort duty** and shelling **shore positions.**

The *Missouri's* nine big 18-inch guns were mounted in three turrets. Other dreadnought class ships had four turrets that could be turned to fire at enemy ships or **emplacements.**

For protection against enemy fire, the *Missouri* had 18 to 22 inches of **armor.** But even with all the big guns and armor, ships in the *Missouri* class could move along at 27 knots.

In 1945, the *Missouri* became famous forever. The top deck of the U.S.S. *Missouri* was the scene of a ceremony in which General Douglas MacArthur and some members of the Japanese government signed an agreement. It was the Japanese surrender ending World War II.

U.S.S. Nautilus

Country: *United States of America*
Class: *Attack submarine*
Launched: *1954*
Length: *323 feet*
Breadth: *27 feet*
Propulsion: *Nuclear power*
Armament: *Six **bow torpedo tubes***

Was the U.S.S. Nautilus *the world's first*
true submarine?

The U.S.S. *Turtle* was the United States Navy's first submarine. The navy even had submarines named *Nautilus* in 1913 and 1930. But none of these were true submarines.

Until 1954, submarines were really **surface** vessels that could work underwater. The *Nautilus* was an *underwater vessel* that could operate on the surface. That made it the world's first true submarine. To demonstrate how long it could stay underwater, the *Nautilus* remained submerged long enough to be the first vessel to travel under the polar icecap from end to end.

The *Nautilus'* nuclear-powered engine can turn out 13,000 **horsepower** for a surface speed of 20 knots. Do sailors on the *Nautilus* have to eat salt pork and dried peas? No, sailors on the *Nautilus* have ice cream and soda bars, a movie theater, libraries, and their own on-board television. About the only thing sailors on this submarine don't have is a field for playing baseball. Yes, the *Nautilus* is a great ship in a great navy.

U.S.S. Enterprise

Country: *United States of America*
Class: *Aircraft carrier*
Commissioned: *November, 1961*
Length: *1123 feet*
Breadth: *257 feet at the **beam***
Propulsion: *Nuclear power*
Complement: *Crew of 4000, 90 aircraft*

U.S.S. Enterprise CVN-65. What does all that mean?

It means the *Enterprise* is a nuclear-powered aircraft carrier named after the *Enterprise,* a conventionally-powered carrier the United States once had.

What about CVN-65? *CV* is the navy **designation** for aircraft carrier. The designation *N* tells us the vessel is nuclear-powered. 65? This is a **hull** number the navy uses. It means the *Enterprise* is the 65th aircraft carrier to be commissioned by the United States Navy.

But what can the *Enterprise* do? We know it can carry a crew of 4000 along with 90 aircraft. Since it is nuclear-powered, it can also go 207,000 miles without refueling. That's about eight trips around the world using nothing but some lumps of **uranium** for fuel.

Not bad, U.S.S. *Enterprise,* CVN-65. Keep up the great work. After all, you are the largest warship in history.

U.S.S. Long Beach

Country: *United States of America*
Class: *Cruiser*
Launched: *July 14, 1959*
Displacement: *17,000 tons, full load*
Propulsion: *Nuclear power*
Armament: *All **missiles***

All missiles? Nothing else?

The U.S.S. *Long Beach* was the first United States cruiser to carry *almost* all missile armaments. Even more important is the fact that the *Long Beach* is the first nuclear-powered surface warship in the United States **arsenal.** Here's a list of the missiles the *Long Beach* carries.

> One twin talos **SAM launcher**
> Two twin terrier standard ER SAM launchers
> Eight tube **ASM** launchers
> Two triple 12.7 inch SMK torpedo tubes

When the navy looked over this list of armaments, they decided to add two single 5″ .38 **cal** guns.

The ship needs 1,081 **enlisted men** and 79 **officers** to run her. The *Long Beach* is like another ship, the huge *Enterprise*. They both have what is called "billboard **radar**" in a block around the **superstructure.** This is a **fixed** radar so no one has to watch it turn.

U.S.S. Boston

Country: *United States of America*
Class: *Cruiser*
Launched: *May 26, 1942*
Displacement: *17,500 tons*
Speed: *35 knots*

A very fast Boston *Terrier?*

No, not at first. During World War II, the *Boston* operated as a heavy cruiser. Her 143-ton gun turret **downed** many a Japanese **Zero.**

Then after World War II, the *Boston* was **refitted** to be the world's first missile-carrying ship. Now the *Boston* became ready to be a Terrier, a ship that launches anti-aircraft Terrier missiles.

Boston has two missile launchers which can fire two Terriers at once. That means the *Boston* can launch four missiles in less than a second. Is there more?

Yes, besides the missiles, the *Boston* has six 8-inch guns, ten 9-inch guns, and twelve more anti-aircraft guns. That seems like plenty of bite for a *"Boston Terrier."*

Armaments

Fists	Swords, knives, daggers
Rocks	Rifles and pistols
Sticks	Cannons
Spears and axes	Torpedoes
Boiling oil	Aircraft
Bows and arrows	Machine guns
Torches	**Depth charges** and **mines**

Naval armaments, from fists to **smart, nuclear-tipped** missiles.

It must have been thousands of years ago. Two people out floating on logs may have gotten into a fight about who could fish where. All of a sudden fists became naval armaments. But naval warfare has changed since those old "fist-in-the-face" days. Since then, people have fought with sticks and stones, rocks, and rockets. During the days of wooden ships, sailors shot burning torches at each other. The torches set sails, ropes, even people on fire. When, during battle, some people tried to climb aboard your ship to capture it, you could douse them with boiling water or oil. That was good news for the fish. Deep fried enemy for lunch!

As years have gone by, weapons have become more **sophisticated.** Countries keep coming up with new ideas. But it seems no one country can stay ahead very long. Still, history shows that naval battles are won by those who make the biggest bang. And a smart, nuclear-tipped weapon could make one big bang, indeed— maybe the last bang in naval warfare?

Propulsion

Water Currents	Steam
Hands	**Diesel**
Paddles	Gasoline
Wind	Nuclear power

Is propulsion all that important?

Propulsion is just as important to warships as armament. After all, if your mighty warship won't move, it's not going to be much good when it's time to go fight the enemy. How did the propulsion part of warships start? Probably when those people on logs used their hands for paddles after they used their fists for the fight.

Thousands of years ago, people discovered that wind would move a ship if you put up a sail. Then in 1769 James Watt discovered the steam engine. That put the galley slaves out of work. Later Dr. Rudolph Diesel invented the diesel engine. That almost put the gasoline-powered engine, invented by Nicholas Otto out of work. Now it appears that nuclear power could put a lot of diesel engines out of work. And what's coming next? Some say there could be still more ways to power a ship. What do you think?

Bismarck Kit

Country: *Germany*
Scale: *About 1:570*

How was the Bismarck *named? Is it a good beginner's kit?*

This German battleship was named after the first Chancellor of the German Empire, Prince Otto Von Bismarck. Is that why it's not a good kit for a beginner?

No, the *Bismarck* is not a good kit for a beginner because it's a big kit with many pieces. If you are a beginner, start with a very simple kit. The U.S.S. *Nautilus* on page 26 is a good kit for a start.

To get started you need a few things besides the kit. You'll need a good place to work. Try to find a place where your kit building won't be in the way and where you can leave your work laid out until it's finished.

You need glue, some paints, a sharp knife, and a piece of sandpaper. Sometimes kit parts have little bumps at the edges where they have been joined with other parts. Sand these bumps off so your model will look neat. After you've made your start with a simple kit, you may be ready for a kit like the *Bismarck*.

If you build a *Bismarck* kit, it may be about 1:570 scale. That means the real *Bismarck* was 570 times bigger than a kit model. If you want to measure the real *Bismarck* to get your scale exact, you'll have to read page 41 to find out where it is.

Bismarck

Country: *Germany*
Launched: *Early 1939*
Length: *791 feet*
Width: *118 feet*
Top speed: *Over 30 knots*
Armaments: *Eight 15-inch guns*

Some said the Bismarck *was unsinkable.*
Were these people right?

During the early years of World War II, the mighty *Bismarck* sailed the seas and sank many British merchant ships. The British navy people decided this must come to an end. It was time to sink the unsinkable *Bismarck.* A spy on the shore of Norway told the British navy where the *Bismarck* was located.

Then two British aircraft spotted the giant ship. All British warships near the *Bismarck* were ordered into battle. "Sink the *Bismarck!*" was the command. Two of Britain's best ships, the *Hood* and the *Prince of Wales,* found the *Bismarck.* The battle started with a shot from the British. The *Bismarck* fired back. The *Hood* was sunk in minutes, and the *Bismarck* steamed away.

Two days later some British aircraft found the *Bismarck* and bombed it. This damage caused the *Bismarck* to slow down. Other ships now started to torpedo the German battleship. The *Bismarck* could no longer fight back. But it still didn't sink.

Finally, beaten, battered, and on fire, the *Bismarck* was torpedoed at close range by two British cruisers. The British navy had carried out its duty. The unsinkable *Bismarck* sank slowly to the bottom of the sea where it joined thousands of other ships which some people had also said were unsinkable.

Warships

Galleys

Galleons

Battleships

Cruisers

Nuclear-Powered

Submarines

Raiders

Have we seen them all?

No, we haven't seen them all. We have seen just a few models because for many years, people have built, sailed, and sunk thousands of warships of all kinds, sizes, and styles. And there are still many warships being planned, designed, and built right now.

Will we ever see them all? Some people say that after a while naval warfare will be obsolete. These people say it's time to scrap the **flattops,** battlewagons, and cruisers. These people say, "All we really need are submarines."

Some say that in a few years, we won't need a navy at all because if there is a war, it will be fought in space. A navy isn't much use in a space war.

Others say as long as people sail the seas, countries will need navies and warships for protection. Maybe that's why we still have many warships on the drawing board.

Today, you can build models and study naval history. Someday you might build or sail on a real warship. You may even be the one who has some new ideas about building and sailing warships. And when that time comes, remember what sailors say. "Anchors aweigh!" In the navy, that means, "Let's go!"

Glossary/Index

A.D.   **A**nno **D**omini, a way of numbering years starting with the year one—Before A.D. year 1, years were B.C. **8**

amphibious   capable of going on land or water, **23**

anchor   heavy iron piece attached to a ship by a strong chain, **13, 43**

armament   any kind of fighting equipment such as guns, torpedoes, bombs, **8, 10, 12, 18, 24, 26, 30, 31, 34, 35, 37, 40**

armor   thick metal slabs used for protection, **25**

armor plate   thick metal plates applied to those parts of a warship that need extra protection, **15**

arsenal   place where explosives are stored, **31**

ASM   air-to-surface missile—See *missile.* **31**

B.C.   See *A.D.* **6**

beam   widest part of a ship, **28**

bireme   Roman galley ship with two slaves at each oar—See *galley.* **6, 7**

boilers   containers where water is boiled to make steam for ship propulsion, **17**

bow   front of a ship, **26**

bow torpedo tubes   torpedo firing tubes at the front of the ship, **26**

breadth   the widest part of a ship, **6, 12, 26, 28**

cal, caliber   measure of the size of a bullet or small cannon, **31**

catapult   machine that accelerates an aircraft off the deck of a ship, much like a sling shot, **17, 23**

44

naval warfare	war at sea, **5, 11, 35, 43**
navigation	guiding or steering a ship, **9**
nuclear power, **nuclear-powered**	power from the splitting of the atom; propelled by the splitting of the atom, **4,** **27–31, 36, 37**
nuclear-tipped	having an atomic bomb—See *missile*. **34, 35**
obsolete	old, no longer usable, **15, 43**
officers	on warships, the people who give the orders and tell the crew what do, **31**
plunder	things taken by force, **9**
propulsion	power needed to move a ship, **6, 10, 12, 14,** **18, 26, 28, 30, 36, 37**
radar	radio that can locate distant objects, **31**
raider	in the navy, a ship that makes quick attacks and then leaves quickly, **4, 42**
raiding cruiser	ship designed to make sudden attacks, **14, 15**
ram bow	sharp pointed front part of a ship used to crash into an enemy ship, **7**
range	on ships, usually the distance a ship can travel without refueling, **22**
recoil	force felt at the back of a gun or cannon as it's fired, **11**
reconnaissance	hunting out the enemy or studying what the enemy has for equipment, **23**
refitted	rebuilt, **17, 33**
SAM launcher	machine used to fire SAM missiles—SAM means surface-to-air. **31**
scale	size in relation to another object, **38, 39**
Scandinavia	group of countries in northern Europe, **8, 9**
scout	look at, hunt out—See *reconnaissance*. **15**
seaworthy	strong, easy to handle ship, **9**
service	time of being in the navy or kind of work done in the navy, **14**

shore positions	usually guns or cannons placed on shore—See *emplacements.* **25**
smart	weapon or missile that can find a very special target, **34, 35**
sophisticated	weapon for a very special job—See *smart.* **35**
submerged	underwater, **21, 27**
sub	short for submarine—See *submarine.* **23**
submarine	ship designed to go on and underwater, **20–23, 26, 27, 42**
suet	fat, usually from beef or mutton (sheep), **13**
superstructure	parts of a ship that stand up from the hull—See *hull.* **31**
surface	on the water, not underwater, **27, 31**
torpedo	bomb that travels underwater toward a target, **18, 19, 26, 31, 34, 41**
trireme	Roman ship that had three slaves at each oar—See *bireme.* **7**
true submarine	ship designed to spend most of the time underwater, **26, 27**
turrets	large structures on a ship's hull that hold cannons, **17, 25, 33, 35**
uranium	material from which atomic bombs are made, **29**
vessel	ship or boat, **15, 25, 27, 29**
Viking ships	strong wooden boats used by the Vikings—See *Scandinavia.* **8**
war materiel	all the equipment and supplies needed to carry on war, **15**
water currents	movement or force of water moving, **36**
Zero	Japanese fighter plane in World War II, **33**